Almost Kid

V. A. Sola Smith
Almost Kid

20/20 **EYEWEAR**
PAMPHLET SERIES
2015

First published in 2015 by Eyewear Publishing Ltd
74 Leith Mansions, Grantully Road
London W9 1LJ United Kingdom

Typeset with graphic design by Edwin Smet
Printed in England by Lightning Source
All rights reserved © 2015 *V A Sola Smith*

The right of V A Sola Smith to be identified as author of this work has been asserted in accordance with section 77 of the Copyright, Designs and Patents Act 1988

ISBN 978-1-908998-69-9
WWW.EYEWEARPUBLISHING.COM

Thanks to the team at Eyewear for making this pamphlet appear, and for keeping these poems from the gutter. Equally big thank-yous are owed to the George Fox School Educational Charity, Kingston University and my family and friends for their attempts to keep me from the gutter. Lastly, to Todd for the innumerable kindnesses you have shown me, and for introducing me to the music of Elliot Smith.

*It's simple. You either get it down on paper,
or you jump off a bridge.*

Charles Bukowski

Table of contents

- 9   *Black Art*
- 11   *The Humble Difference Between Horse Radish and Dock*
- 12   *Punchline*
- 13   *Poor Fish*
- 14   *Downside Up*
- 16   *Spare Change*
- 17   *Laggies*
- 18   *Almost Kid*
- 19   *No Tel Motel*
- 20   *Sorry*
- 21   *Tough Tough Tough*
- 23   *Sylvia*
- 24   *Heroin*
- 25   *Bereavement*
- 26   *Exit Fee*
- 27   *Job Seeker*
- 28   *People in Glass Houses*
- 29   *Once Upon a Time...*
- 30   *Reply to the Call of Sunset Over the Trough of Bowland*
- 31   *Grave Digging*

Black Art

Casting a spell with an instruction manual,
radio across his lap, trying to revive his last sacrifice,
an army of curses gossip beneath his breath.

I watch how all his forbidden words lose
their form in the shash of this house, living
room booby-trapped with unspeakables,

the simple flourishing threat of tongues
teeheeing like caged birds. Sunday morning
dunked like a biscuit in the baptism pool of TV.

Dad will disappear anytime now and I left
to the care of a purple dinosaur reciting ABCs.
Aunt Lou, not a blood aunt, but your bingo sister,

and Mrs Number Nineteen, sighing desires into a potion
of tea leaves. A gloss of wide screens like carnival mirrors
distorting, promising, confirming. You crowd

a catalogue, grimoire of wishes, before rushing to pray
at the pay-by-minute altar in the dark beneath the stairs.
Now Dad's been beat and my bothers banished,

it is my turn to try Pandora's Box. And, my luck,
I twist my hand at the dial like a key and
poetry fills the room like magic; words like giants

conquering ranges of cushions
ordered to look disarranged, strange
rhythms spilling and clattering like marbles,

intonations bubbling and toiling,
tempers brooding and bursting like stars
glaring. Mrs Number Nineteen, Aunt Lou and you

soaring over the pop-up, flat pack skyline of furniture,
Formica breakfast bar beneath a shanty slum silhouette of
kitsch, duelling with the power of 'If I could Tell You' –

Dyson, *Disney*, the lure of *McDonald's*, that *Dior* dress,
the hocus pocus of Number Four's *Ford Focus*, and of knowing
folk here would kill for less. I shroud myself in Dad's new court suit,

a magic carpet on higher finance tearing from beneath me
and the radio, its split antennae like rabbit ears, drawn
from my hands, poems like hankies streaming like noses.

You set about bleaching the air with 96.9 FM. Aunt Lou
incantating the latest, tongue wafting like incense:
Mrs So-and-So's missing geraniums, saving the best

for last: Mr You Know Who's lip reader wife. You cackle
like hags – think you've vanished me. Upstairs
to sit pretty like Rapunzel, hair docked like Samson's – nice try,

but I am nobody's ticky-tack princess, nor petrified
prize ornamenting a window; so, princes, don't waste your time,
go save yourselves, for I cannot be won, I am too busy,

busy, sharpening my tongue, eyes hardened to crystal,
little witch, proper; when I am done, pickling, stewing,
I shall draw my own wand, and feel its ink rage like black magic.

The Humble Difference Between Horse Radish and Dock

Mum and Dad met The Relatives at the door,
the way they greeted the filth, not really
a greeting at all; double crossing with kisses
a man like my Dad, who could – and did – kill

a frenzied mutt with a single head-butt,
and my brothers and I with nowt but a look,
and Mum, white witch, who prized tea and afters
and us like tricks from hedgerows by the roadsides –

rash, in more ways than one. Returning the gift,
Dad paltered up a store of patience, set aside
for my brothers and I, whose grind it were
to meantime eye their bairn, begger off awhile,

lark 'mongst the palmates; hunt hogweed, ground elder,
run the sedges, and if the fairies should try their luck
let 'em see how far it gets them, where lizards are legless
and worms have teeth and fairies don't flit so much as leg it

double-quick and egged by natterjack calls,
taking long, loud running jumps through the nettles
and plucking leaves and bulrushes like straws,
sorry as trash caught up in a storm of angel's breath,

pockets pouring like watering cans,
like lint knows how to hush a nettle sting
or else you can somehow bribe the plants to tell.

Punchline

Tin tin tin, get it
or an eawl-leet skryke, t'be sure.
Every beggin' sennet down't pop shop. Pa
yammerin. Tin tin tin is the ring o'life on't strap,
naymind scraps; Mam'll fix bally anne. Ah kid,
tin tin tin, get it now, or 'cross Pa's lap,
punch line's its own joke.

Poor Fish

Shell suits, crushed by the sagging tarpaulin of Asian
fabric stalls, in penny arcades and sneaking to redemption
games beyond the crack exterior of shooting galleries,
and the crack reality of shooting galleries, a whisper

between the isles of bargain basement food stuff stores,
stealing from the ginnells and cobbled snickets, not yet
tripping unseen about their fate like the helter skelter
fun house stairs we rode along the promenade as kids

eager for the night to tear across the shoreline, faceless
and fearless and one against the jetstream of the whole North
Atlantic, bellowing then at each raised hand till it shattered
at our feet, powerless to salt even our sneaker soles,

launching kisses and slaps in the dark, desperate
to pull and push and plummet deeper
and farther into the prize draw rock pools
where the sea spits all the poor fish like shells.

We were just kids, trying our luck against that killer tide,
downing fluorescent alcohol and sparking rough cut green,
careless, rogues seeds whizzing and bursting,
every night, vandalising the ocean's *sssh* approach
like fireworks, raging to break through the bore.

Downside Up
    ...*to Jim Carroll*

There must be millions like us,
tossed off and dropped
penny by penny,

worthless. Yet here
the Metrolink unfolds
its Fagin palm seats

to empty out the pockets
of Greater Manchester.
We ride

the Pied Piper from Ladywell
to Media City UK, a veritable goldmine.
Behind the back of Piccadilly

The Tib Street Horn
and Afflecks Palace
rub shoulders like pimps

in the Northern Quarter.
Dipping into the night
like ink, here I am, again

writing letters to you
on the flipside
of the old Coliseum,

and waiting a dealer's length.
For the brief passing
of your white ship

kids press themselves
like graffiti, like blood
against these alley walls:

rows upon rows of us
abandoned poems
secretly crowding

the back pages of these streets
just to get ripped off,
screwed up.

Spare Change

just crack

beneath the fumes

wings like ash

riding long days

prickle and settle

the city

into fragile street sleep

shattered

with pins and needles

or just the crackling

of stars and lampposts

igniting

cigarettes

with sparks of paranoia

holding out for a light

just begging for change

Laggies

Torn off by a sly cat tongue wind, desire
lines of age'd, achenes
of fine white hair, like dandelion clocks
carried on wishes, memories, prayers, regrets.

Sugar stealers hitch hiking in the hems of pass-me-downs,
we forage the chestnut crowds for laggies, otherwise to be
put to seed by the not-yet mulch of soon-to-be
bluebells, misting the earth in a sudden haze, like confetti

and later, cancer. Scarring the wood, until the autumn
salve of foliage consigns our adventures to the long-time-past,
lile irises like hover flies pog whirlybirds from the ashes,
slight as a breeze through the knells of all the bluebells

to dig bobber nub graveyards. We shoot our mouths
secrets, dirty our language, our selves, burying all the colours
of the rainbow, beyond the long trains of all the dogs'
business dragged through this forest like bodies.

Almost Kid

Background voices compete with mine. What is left
for me, but *you too, you too?* The heating
pre-set to flip when you arrive. Once mine,
you're a voice, I struggle these days to
recognise; Jesus, 'could be anyone –
I try my hardest not to think 'bout it.
Crashing the airwaves, fragments of a gift
double wrapped in hair. And blood. Imposter
of a kid I remember. Crystal clear
photo frames. How thoughtful of you. Fair-
trade too. A disposable camera.
Funny. An envelope loaded with glitter.
Let it lie. Move on. Forget it. A list –
my friends are dying, yours getting divorced –
adult trumps. You're not a kid anymore.
I let you win, anyway. That's my job.
A cleaned-out ice cream tub filled with Brussels.
I offer you a dead bird, Yorkshires, spread
condiments like gold, frankincense and myrrh.
We sit either side of a palisade,
tallying false-starts. Chrome pepper grinder
like a cenotaph. Ignored. Untouched.
A Tupperware of cranberry jelly.
Pulling crackers, setting our crowns aside
and reciting the punch lines of bad jokes,
deconstructing systematically
that awkward half-hug-half-handshake, half-laugh-
half-shrug at the door – almost, kid. But then
I'm alone, again. Half drunk, half dreaming…
did I ask you for that game of charades?

No Tel Motel
...for Laurie

On a raised platform, three beds, quite simply
arranged, like the stage of a Harold Pinter play.
We are the only things good-for-nothing in this room.

You drag the coffee table like a reluctant dog,
fingers beneath its rigid collar, lay it at my knees.
My hand explores its matted fur. Last night's rogue fleas,

toast crumbs, cigarette ash and some white dust, vit-c perhaps,
proof of things that cannot just be said, like how I get scared
every time. Even now. Especially now.

Spoon arched, prickling to a hiss and sputter,
breath, overwhelming the tongue sponge of a q-tip,
I pin it down. Evidence of my virgin technique

lingering like the inscription of lovers' initials.
They say every killer has his signature – and his price.
Mine writes itself in the copse where I bury my point

devastating the landscape of your body.
Your red hair puddling onto a pillow, like your body is
actually dissolving. In time it will curl, climb

itself, like it too cannot bear to touch down,
shedding the weight of what has been done to it.
But for now, you just wobble a rock of white

back and forth between the black smirks
scheming beneath your fingernails. In the ditch
of your arm, the mouth of a fledgling tongue.

Sorry

I am harkened, little roar,
each floorboard's sigh,
hesitating by my closed door,
the offer of coffee, freeze dried.

Tough Tough Tough

It was quite a shock, first observing how
my flourishes of awe bled and wilted
when I pressed them against gauze,
those early attempts, the cross section of a scream;

my petals curling inwards, closing in on me,
a budding chain of knuckle and knot; a flower
whose carpel, its iodine stains, whispered;
I love you – not. Secretly reaching for your lips,

trembling like butterfly wings, bewitching
that brown, tumorous, liquorish roll-up like a fuse
in the cherry bomb of your fist, mottled pink,
symmetrical nicotine blotches, shaped like lungs.

It's no wonder I became a murderer, picking off
feelings like scabs and later, a chain smoker,
flicking off the empty butts of brown roaches,
and cremating my dead ends in the ornate ashtrays

of public gardens; pig tape waving like may pole ribbons,
burning memories into the knots of my own
folded arms. Snuffing out the double rage
of broken homes and single parents,

tending to morning glories,
bruising beneath the weight of creepers,
unscrewing wedding rings. All those disappointed *oh*s:
a perennial runaway,

later, with your seed planted in my mouth.
I've spent a lot of time drawing splinters like short straws,

thinking of that butterfly – my first voodoo,
until I made myself my own voodoo doll.

My teens were seven years of trying
to feel anything, except that first shock
of having to shift bodies, cradling the dead-heads
of my mother's efforts; a smear of lipstick,

a cold sore, the sovereign of my brother's lips,
dark places where I felt safest because no one could
try save me. But even the grave spat me out
like the womb, pink and red and somehow yellow. Funny,

how my eyes stammer open, again and again
and again. Tether of veins like an umbilical cord,
shrouded in blood stained tape like shredded
tobacco, expertly double rolled

into a tight little chrysalis, quite plain,
in fact. My best attempt yet.
I cannot resist peeling the gauze like brown paper
and lifting the scab; look,

what Death has made me:
a small, pale pinkish bloom;
not quite pretty…
but *tough, tough, tough.*

Sylvia

You were a panzer, horrifyingly
technical in your approach,
thin armoured, yet a panzerkampfwagen

no less. You bit off two wars,
one famously; you pocked its cheek
with your fire. You knew how to kiss

and you were hungry, more
ravenous. Your artillery swelled
with the insatiable promise of life's loss,

you became awesome. More, now
your death drive was astounding.
My wheels get stuck. I find myself

stopped in your tracks, immobilised,
a useless model death machine of your design.
Once, I too was a glad victim. Of the men you've killed,

I feel too. Only, I cannot say I do.
Ich, I cannot kill, nor be. Your ghost
tyre marks tyrannize page after page.

Heroin

I have visions of washing back
my reflection,
red carpet; trail of a tourniquet
slipping away
in favour of a Valentino;
nodding off, an award
in my fist, not a needle;
Johnny Depp setting fire to the bed
tonight, instead of a cigarette.
I dream the sound
of having already scored
and of splitting
a six figure paycheque,
purr revving like a Jag
gearing up
to roar.

Bereavement

It is a deep ache not a slight sting,
a warm rush, when it first worms in.

The blood travels like a defiant arm
through the debris of an earthquake,

shattering easy as a city
nature tidies up like toys.

Exit Fee

Pig cars sponge the puddle like a trough. At their feet,
the cool palm that rubbed your face in the smut of another day's
ashes, smudging the circus costume of this city's flesh. Now
just a memory; the glimmer of a coin, hollow as a ring.
Red men shoot their flash lights. Stop! U-turn.

Expressions of No Entry, converge, give way,
where disused train tracks like leather belt scars
cross out via a fresh slash of railings. Unfamiliar
faces break out like disease, rain closing in on the cobbles,
brown teeth, edged in blood. Her old corner smirks

the ironic grin of a skull prized from a girl,
you were just trying to show a little love.

Job Seeker

Time becomes a sickening loop-the-loop, days of
defying the phone pressed by you to spew:

wait for that voice to seep through the queue
fug of smoke and break downs: your worn out
slippers hissing *shurrup, shurrup, shurrup…*

when the phone lows into being, a quick hustle to
bring, bring. Bank details, I.D. white shirt, black shoes.
And *smile.* Rider of the one-track-not-so-merry-go-round,

we are delighted to inform – you
hold on tight and prepare to scream.

People in Glass Houses

Old women on buses do it.
Drunk men in nightclub bars
who only in the dark dare to
draw up like bad ideas, do it.
Mothers at baby groups do it.
Interviewers always do it.
Nurses do it, whose job it is
to take bloods and talk cures.
Doctors whilst taking blood pressure,
bored teens in roller coaster queues and
couples who kiss and lark in supermarkets too.
A tattoo artist once did it with a needle
travelling like a missile towards my wrist.
Yet, few are ever brave enough to
just ask. If you did, I'd tell it: explain how
balls are earned, but stones are given.

Once Upon a Time...

Whose window was it you stood at like a bride?
Everyday its own big day, only you didn't know it
then. Whose face sleepy yawned at your close?
Whose naked fingers pressed themselves like birthday candles
burning against your mute folds like lips to be snuffed, blown out?
And what did those hands go on to do – except your undoing,
who knows? How many blackouts you withstood,
in the way of this world, if not to dry out then to hang,
unravelling, fraying, falling apart, but never telling,
a graceful sentinel, never crumpling, but waiting
and without asking, without expecting, unassuming,
never hopeless and never hoping.

How many children did you once guard against this monster
darkness come now, scattering seekers, giggles like rainbows
rolling and clattering out of reach in bubbles hard as marbles,
to wink beneath the sun of each morning,
splitting you in two for the hundredth time, what did this to you;
who faded you, siphoned your colour like blood?

Not just the sun, concealer stained hands, or father, tearing you back
to square up to things only a drunk can – only a drunk can't;
flinching without flinching – what an art;
road side suckling at the puddles of your wounds.
Someone once thought you worthy
of some place in their private space, kingdom
of a bedroom or children's nursery,
guarding their kids, absorbing their love like spills,
keeping their secrets. Still, now
they have had enough of hiding behind you,
I pull you close, lying beneath your weight,
and dream. I knew them too...

A Reply to the Call of Sunset Over the Trough of Bowland

Words charge their rhythms like cavalry.
Ingleborough, Wernside, Pen-y-ghent,
once introduced to me as if God's

Wise Men. There is no forgetting
mature heather's hue of bruises
branding those mountains. Necrotic

black, the colour of summer. After
every greasy brown spring of new blood,
autumn. Ewe mothers' bleating confusion.

Winter dawns, the sun turning violet
on the snow. A crushing impression.
Children rush to dirty the untouched

tabulae rasae of fields. Letters to God
stamped with the seal of snow
angels, decomposing in the rain.

Grave Digging

1 – You were the first
dead person I ever saw.
I was eight months old
and I don't remember you.
You died of cancer just before
we got colour television.

2 – One day, without explanation,
they tore us apart like a fortune cookie,
like breaking us could break *us* – make me tell
the truth; tell them what makes a person
do such a thing – *love* such a thing.
At your wake, I snaked their shins like black grasses,
burrowing beneath the white linen of buffet tables,
tiny hands laden with cocktail onions,
and misunderstanding.

3 – The last thing I said to you was, *I hope you die*.
You shouldn't have bottled my then boyfriend, and
you shouldn't have run into the road without looking
both ways. Sorry, was not enough, and will never be now.

4 – You told me to always wear a seatbelt
and to never ride with Trix, if he's been drinking.
Your parents held your funeral at the school chapel,
I didn't go, but watched them all enter and exit
from a floor above, like I had died,
body stuck as if nailed into my row, and pupils
pointlessly skimming over mourners like souls
studding the black Styx of tarmac below. And afterwards,
while they were busy uselessly crying, *what the hell
were you thinking?*, I rode with Trix.

5 – You were the only friend I've ever had
who didn't in some way call death's bluff.
Perhaps that's why death took its time with you,
tasking its clumsy apprentice to perform a post-mortem
while you were still alive. Fumbling about
your brain like a rolodex, like somehow it kept thinking
it had knocked upon the wrong door.
I bet if you'd have known God's plans for you
you'd have took that joint – always offered you,
just in case, had more of those 'one last drinks',
maybe even tried overcome your fear of needles,
before you had no choice,
before even the drugs couldn't save you.

6 – The image of strangers
scooping you up like a broken piñata
and on your birthday, while we were all waiting
in the literal dark on the otherside,
a chorus of paused 'surprise' – that back fired.
The ambulance arrived to find you already thirty
feet from your car, your cheek rouged
from your long brush with the concrete.
They said you were still clutching your blusher.
I still can't figure if that's irony.

7 – Your mother found you hanging
in the house where we played mums and dads
as children. She gave your dog away
the morning your ex admitted it;
the baby was yours. Your mother thinks
if you'd have known, you'd still be alive.
I'm glad you did it when you only had
the simple love of one bitch to kill.

8 –Now I am done digging, don't you
have something set aside for me? After all,
I have done your dirty work.
Got the scars plain as a paper trail,
and for what? To earn my place
amongst clowns instead of angels
where loves are forced to hide like lies –
some paradise that is, where love is no use
to me, until I've no use for love.
Fuck that. And fuck you. I might as well
be dead – truly; make my halo a gun
if life is just a spade; I'm done
digging. I quit, if that is all there is
to love, if heaven is my only wage,
Jesus Christ, let the devil dig my grave.

Acknowledgements are due to the editors of *Lung Jazz: Young British Poets for Oxfam* and *Sculpted: an Anthology of the North West*, where versions of 'Sylvia', 'Poor Fish' and 'Downside Up' have appeared.

 **EYEWEAR** PUBLISHING

EYEWEAR
20/20
PAMPHLET
SERIES

BEN STAINTON EDIBLES
MEL PRYOR DRAWN ON WATER
MICHAEL BROWN UNDERSONG
MATT HOWARD THE ORGAN BOX
RACHAEL M NICHOLAS SOMEWHERE NEAR IN THE DARK
BETH TICHBORNE HUNGRY FOR AIR
GALE BURNS OPAL EYE
PIOTR FLORCZYK BAREFOOT
LEILANIE STEWART A MODEL ARCHAEOLOGIST
SHELLEY ROCHE-JACQUES RIPENING DARK
SAMANTHA JACKSON SMALL CRIES
V.A. SOLA SMITH ALMOST KID
GEORGE SZIRTES NOTES ON THE INNER CITY
JACK LITTLE ELSEWHERE
DAMILOLA ODELOLA LOST & FOUND
KEITH JARRETT I SPEAK HOME

Printed by Libri Plureos GmbH in Hamburg, Germany